THE
ESSENTIALS
TRUTHS FROM JESUS'S GREATEST SERMON

MW01125015

ISBN 978-1-0877-4837-5
Item 005833495
Dewey Decimal Classification Number: 242
Subject Heading: DEVOTIONAL LITERATURE / BIBLE STUDY AND TEACHING / GOD

Printed in the United States of America

Student Ministry Publishing
Lifeway Resources
200 Powell Place, Suite 100,
Brentwood, TN 37027-7514

We believe that the Bible has God for its author; salvation for its end; and truth, without any mixture of error, for its matter and that all Scripture is totally true and trustworthy. To review Lifeway's doctrinal guideline, please visit www.lifeway.com/doctrinalguideline.

PUBLISHING TEAM

Director, Student Ministry
Ben Trueblood

Manager, Student Ministry Publishing
John Paul Basham

Editorial Team Leader
Karen Daniel

Writer
Jay Watson

Content Editor
Kyle Wiltshire

Production Editor
Brooke Hill

Cover Design
Kaitlin Redmond

Graphic Designer
Shiloh Stufflebeam

TABLE OF CONTENTS

4
intro

5
getting started

6
the heart

40
the how

74
the hope

108
a little upside down

110
the heart:
the root of it all

INTRO

In today's world, people often say they like Jesus; they just don't like religion. They feel that He is kinder and gentler than the Old Testament and goes to battle against the judgmental nature of religious people and churches. The reality is, Jesus wasn't too fond of that type of religion either. Don't believe it? Check out the Sermon on the Mount.

The Sermon on the Mount was Jesus's longest recorded sermon. In this teaching, He spoke against people who did good things just so others would see them. He also revealed the heart behind every major teaching the Old Testament offered. Jesus said, "Don't think that I came to abolish the Law or the Prophets. I did not come to abolish but to fulfill" (Matt. 5:17).

Jesus not only revealed the heart of what God intends for people who follow Him, but Jesus fully and completely followed through on every word He spoke. Jesus addressed the heart of anger, lust, keeping promises, and just about every form of daily living. He talked about building a faith upon a rock-solid foundation—that foundation being Himself—and not just His teachings, but His life, ministry, death, and resurrection. Knowing that Jesus died to forgive the sins of the world helps His followers to be faithful in practicing forgiveness. Jesus cared about true, authentic, faithful living.

This devotion is not for the faint of heart. It will challenge your perceptions of not only what you do for Christ, but why you do it. It will teach you how Jesus wants you to pray. It will remind you that there are two choices: a wide path or a narrow path. One path is easy and crowded but leads to destruction. The other path is much more difficult but leads to life. You may have heard most or all of these teachings of Jesus in the past, but have you actively chosen to understand how you can live them out? The good news is that Jesus is calling you to ask, seek, and knock. If you truly hunger to understand the righteousness of God, you will be blessed.

GETTING STARTED

This devotional contains 30 days of content, broken down into sections. Each day is divided into three elements—discover, delight, and display—to help you answer core questions related to Scripture.

discover |

This section helps you examine the passage in light of who God is and determine what it says about your identity in relationship to Him. Included here is the daily Scripture reading, focus passage, along with illustrations and commentary to guide you as you explore God's Word.

delight |

In this section, you'll be challenged by questions and activities that help you see how God is alive and active in every detail of His Word and your life. We've given you a whole page to write your answers to these questions, so really think and dig in.

display |

Here's where you take action. Display calls you to apply what you've learned through each day's devotion.

> **Each day also includes a prayer activity at the conclusion of the devotion.**

Throughout the devotional, you'll also find other resources to help you connect with the topic, such as Scripture memory verses, additional resources, and articles that help you go deeper into God's Word.

SECTION 1

THE HEART

As your heart beats, blood flows through it and pumps life through your entire body. Without a working heart, you can't survive. The same can be said about your spiritual heart—the part of you that no one knows but you and God. Your heart is the center of your will, emotions, and thoughts. Your heart is symbolic of what you believe. You can say you have faith in God, but do you mean it? In this section, we'll see Jesus calling people to the true heart of following God.

BLESSED

discover |

READ MATTHEW 5:3-10.

*"Blessed are those who hunger and thirst for righteousness,
for they will be filled." —Matthew 5:6*

Have you ever wondered what Jesus meant when He used the word
"Blessed"? Chapters 5-7 in Matthew are called the Sermon on the
Mount. This was Jesus showing the world what it actually means to "be"
a Christian. He was describing what happens when you give your life to
Him. "Blessed" in this case meant to have mature character and faith.

Verses 3-10 tell a story with verse 6 as the turning point. It is a before
and after description. Verses 3-5 describe realizing your need for Christ:
poor in spirit, mourning, and meek. We are weak without Jesus; we
should mourn the sin in our life, and the reality of our weakness and
meekness cause us to realize we are truly broken and in need of saving.
In verse 6, you find the word hunger. This type of hunger is a longing to
be made right by Jesus. The only way we can experience salvation and
peace is through faith in Jesus. He alone makes us righteous.

When we are saved, our lives should look different. We show mercy
to people because we have been shown mercy. Our hearts long for
the things of God and not the things of this world. Because Jesus has
brought us peace within, we want to make peace with others. This text
basically says this: You need Jesus because you are broken. Only Jesus
can make you right. Your life must look different because of Jesus.

delight |

Take a moment and think about what it means to mourn over the sin in your life. How does this brokenness reveal your need for Jesus?

How can you practice mercy, a pure heart, and peacemaking today?

display |

Maybe you've read these verses a few times before and thought that you'd never be able to live up to what God's calling you to do. That's the beauty of it. Jesus tells us that we need Him, and giving our lives to Christ in faith is life-changing. His mercy, truth, and peacemaking cause us to want to do the same. Take a moment and write a before and after list of your life before Christ and after. It is amazing to see what Jesus has already done by leading you toward mature character.

BEFORE	AFTER

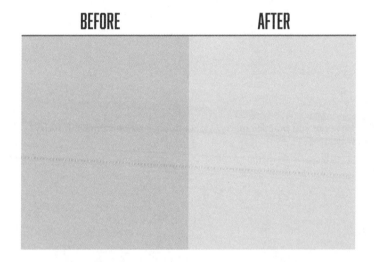

Is it possible that you've never spent a lot of time thinking about what your life was like before Christ and then how exactly you are supposed to live as a Christian? Take some time in prayer and talk to God about your need for Him. Thank Him for saving you, bringing you peace, and making you right in His eyes. Finally, pray for God to show you how you can help others see Him through your mercy, purity, and peacemaking. If you've never given Jesus your life, what is stopping you from doing that today?

PAIN & GAIN

discover |

READ MATTHEW 5:11-12.

*"You are blessed when they insult you and persecute you and
falsely say every kind of evil against you because of me. Be glad
and rejoice, because your reward is great in heaven. For that is
how they persecuted the prophets who were before you."*

Jesus told us one of the results of living a "blessed" life is persecution
and suffering. In fact, He explicitly stated that we should rejoice over this.
What would you be willing to endure for the cause of Christ?

Jesus's words were very personal. He did not infer that some distant,
unknowable folks in another place would be insulted and persecuted. He
said "you." This blessing specifically comes from suffering on His behalf.
In other words, if you suffer because of your actions for Christ, you will
be blessed. Your blessing will also be heavenly and eternal.

In lots of ways, that doesn't make it easier in the moment. There will be
times when you will suffer because of your relationship with Jesus and
desire to follow Him. Maybe you'll lose friends, maybe you'll lose out on
opportunities, and maybe it will cause pain in your heart and life.

Do not forget, though, when you genuinely give your life to Jesus, a
process of transformation begins. The forgiveness you've been shown
brings peace and causes you to hunger after the things of God. This
blessing is only topped by the gift of eternity in heaven with Jesus. His
blessings are everlasting, not temporary.

delight

How have you experienced suffering because of Christ?

How do you remain encouraged even when you face insults and persecution for following after Jesus?

display |

There are two ways this passage could be a little scary. One comes from considering suffering that might happen. The other is talking about death and eternity. If you combine these two thoughts, it means that you could give up your life because of your faith. This world is not our home, and we are called to live differently because of Jesus. This is the "blessed" life. What would you be willing to endure for the cause of Christ? How can you choose His righteousness no matter the outcome today? Below, write out one way you have chosen to follow Christ, regardless of the outcome. Then, write out one way you would like to choose to follow Christ, regardless of the outcome.

The entire concept of prayer is submission. You are telling God that He is in charge of everything all the time. In your submission you are developing your relationship with God. It is for you to learn to trust Him and give Him everything. Right now, rather than praying about your potential suffering, pray that God will help you to trust Him and live righteously no matter what comes of it. Ask God how you can make choices that will honor Him regardless of the outcome.

SALTY & LIT

discover |

READ MATTHEW 5:13-16.

"You are the light of the world. A city situated on a hill cannot be hidden."—Matthew 5:14

Ever had French fries with no salt? Talk about disgusting! Today, we use salt to make food taste good, and it makes a substantial impact. In Jesus's time, salt was used to protect meat from spoiling too soon. It helped keep the meat from going bad. Jesus said we are to be like salt.

He also calls us light. It is interesting to think that the only reason a room is dark is simply because there is no light. We can't create darkness, it's just what happens when there is no light. But when light shows up, it invades everything around it. It can't be avoided. Like a city on a hill, we are the light of the entire planet.

These are exciting illustrations that describe an active Christian faith. The "blessed" life. Salty and lit. All of it points to choices we make every day to honor Jesus. The way we speak, the way we care for people around us, and general acts of goodness and kindness aren't just things we do, they are salt—helping to season the world with goodness. They are light—crushing the darkness.

For the follower of Jesus, this is an inescapable destiny. You can't hide light. The result of this blessed life is that the world will see the good things you do and it will be a picture of how Jesus has saved you. These good things bring God glory.

delight

As you think about the importance of this text, make it personal. How has God brought salt and light into your world?

Most likely, the salt and light God brought into your world had a face and name. Who are some people you have found to be amazing examples of Jesus to you? How did they model Christlikeness to you?

display |

Let's take salt and light and compare them to specific words that often define Christianity. Let's make salt forgiveness and light love.

As you have been forgiven by Christ, how can you forgive others to help them see what Christ has done? Forgiveness isn't natural to this world, but when people do it, it radically changes the "flavor" of any situation. What are some ways you can forgive others around you?

If light is love, the sacrificial love of Jesus is transforming you. His act of love was dying for us. How can you lay your life down for others as an act of love?

Ask the Holy Spirit to help you make a list. Write down 20 ways you can specifically show forgiveness and love to your world. For the forgiveness choices, write salt next to them. For the acts of love, write light next to those. Finally, ask God to change the hearts of the people in your world.

MORE THAN LOOKING RIGHT

discover |

READ MATTHEW 5:17-20.

*"Do not think that I have come to abolish the Law or the Prophets;
I have not come to abolish but to fulfill."—Matthew 5:17*

Jesus didn't look right. He did lots of things that most other Jewish teachers and leaders wouldn't do. He spent time talking with women and people who were known as "sinners" to the rest of the Jewish community. He would have meals with them. Because of this, there were always questions about how He operated under God's laws.

Sometimes people do the right things—even great things—because of how it looks. Sometimes people do good things the right way because they don't want to get caught. Jesus had a different motivation for doing righteous things even though they didn't look right. These four verses directly address what Jesus thought about God's law. He knew it was perfect, and He perfectly fulfilled it.

In verse 19, He talked about both teaching and doing. Whoever does these things and teaches them will be rewarded greatly in the kingdom of heaven. Jesus was talking about right motivation for the right reasons. The next several verses in the chapter will get to the heart of each issue. In no way did Jesus ever diminish the Old Testament law of God. In fact, He took it a step farther: He followed the heart of God's laws perfectly.

delight |

The law and the words of the prophets were written for us to understand who God is and how we are supposed to live to honor Him. If Jesus came to fulfill them, what do you think that means?

How does knowing Jesus help us to understand how we are supposed to live?

display |

Jesus wasn't motivated by fear. He didn't worry about doing the right things for the wrong reasons. Why do you do good things? Do you act rightly so that people will think you are good? Do you make good choices hoping that God will bless you because of those choices? If your motivation is selfish, then what's the point of doing good?

God is calling you to do good things and honor God's laws because of the salvation that comes from Jesus fulfilling His law. Because of Jesus, He calls us to live like Jesus.

Write out 2-3 ideas of how you can do the right thing this week, even if no one knows. Then follow up and do these right things.

Ask God to show you the ways you are doing good things for the wrong reasons. Pray about your desires to bring a spotlight to your actions for selfish reasons. Ask God to help you live for Him because of what Jesus has done.

As a specific example, pray for God to show you ways to obey Him through good works of love without anyone knowing that it was you that did it. Ask God to remind you of what Jesus has done for you out of selflessness.

The Essentials

GASOLINE OR WATER?

discover |

READ MATTHEW 5:21-26.

"But I tell you, everyone who is angry with his brother or sister will be subject to judgment. Whoever insults his brother or sister, will be subject to the court. Whoever says, 'You fool!' will be subject to hellfire."—Matthew 5:22

Do you enjoy a good bonfire? When you go to put out the fire at the end of the night, do you use gasoline or water? The answer seems simple, right? But we don't always make that same choice in life. When it comes to heated situations, we can pour on the gasoline of anger and make it grow or we can throw on it the water of forgiveness and put it out before it spreads.

Most everyone agrees that murder is wrong. Furthermore, we are all pretty thankful this is one of God's laws that all find acceptable. It brings a certain amount of safety to our minds. This is evidence of how Jesus came not to abolish God's laws, but to fulfill them. He talked about the fire that can cause murder.

Misplaced anger can lead to hatred. That hatred, if enough gasoline is poured on it, can not only lead to a murderous heart, but to actions that can't be taken away. Jesus wants His followers to be mindful of what anger can do to ourselves and others in our lives.

A Christ-follower is responsible for putting out the fires of hatred that lead to murder. A Christ-follower must strive to bring peace to people around them because Jesus is the ultimate bringer of peace.

delight |

There are different kinds of anger. Think about the few times Jesus got angry in the New Testament. Now think about the times you get angry. Is your anger about people dishonoring God (like Jesus's was), or is it about you being slighted or wronged in some way?

If anger comes from pride, then what are a few ways you can put water on the fires in your heart?

display |

Jesus told His followers ways to combat a murderous heart. The first was to examine any anger that leads to hatred in your own heart and put it out. The second was to be an active "firefighter of hatred" in the lives of others. Jesus directly called them to go to the person they'd offended and make it right.

This is one of the best ways to showcase the way that Jesus has made you a new creation. Laying down your own pride and anger for the sake of helping others to put out hate in their hearts is a world-changing action. This is the sacrificial love of Jesus on display for the world. It would be like carrying water buckets in both hands. Today, as a symbol, find a small travel bottle for shampoo or some other small item that can hold liquid. Fill it up with water and put it in a place where you will see it often. Let it remind you to put water on the fires of anger in your heart.

Take some time and reflect on things that have made you angry in your past. Then ask the Holy Spirit to reveal to you why you got angry. Was your anger about something that dishonored God, or was it something that came from selfish motivation? Ask God to help you to put out the fires in your own heart.

DAY 6

PURE MIND, PURE HEART

discover |

READ MATTHEW 5:27-30.

"You have heard that it was said, 'You shall not commit adultery.' But I say to you that everyone who looks at a woman lustfully has already committed adultery with her in his heart."—Matthew 5:27–28

It was normal in New Testament Jewish culture for most people to be married before the age of 20. It is difficult to imagine this today. Because of being married at such a young age, sex before marriage wasn't as large of an issue as was adultery. Adultery is either a husband or a wife choosing to have a sexual relationship with someone outside of their marriage. This is also one of the Ten Commandments. It is clearly important to God.

Jesus, as with murder and hatred, revealed the heart of the law through His teaching. He said that if you even imagine having a sexual relationship with someone who is not your spouse, it would be the same as actually committing adultery in God's eyes.

Jesus's teaching isn't just a way to avoid sexual sin. It's an attack on contentment, coveting (wanting something that's not yours), and an escape to sinful places in your imagination. The answer Jesus gave for protection? It was vivid imagery of violently removing the problem. If your eye causes you to sin, pluck it out! If your hand causes sin, cut it off! While Jesus didn't literally mean these things, He was very clear about the importance of the mind and sexual sin and how important it was to flee from it.

The Essentials

delight |

Have you ever thought about contentment and lust being connected? How do you think lust points to you not being content?

God designed marriage to be a lifelong commitment, in which a man and a woman give their lives to each other, only sharing their bodies with each other, promising to love and honor each other until death separates them. Even though you are probably years away from marriage, how does lust harm this future commitment in your life?

Lifeway Students | Devotions 24

display |

To be clear, Jesus wasn't talking about recognizing and appreciating beauty in a person of the opposite gender. It is God who created us and very specifically created sex and marriage for His purposes. Healthy sexuality in a marriage relationship is exactly what God intended. Lusting after other people can only cause harm.

Here is a good example for your personal life: There are many cars that drive on the street, but you have complete control over who you allow to park in the driveway of your home. The driveway belongs to you.

Your mind is a place where you control what happens. Yes, beauty is everywhere, but you have control over what you think, how you think it, what you look at, and how you look at it. Fight to control your thoughts to honor God. It's your driveway.

Allow the Holy Spirit to help you to make a prayerful list of all the attributes you want in a future spouse. Make your list as specific as you'd like. Study your list and then think about how you can prepare yourself to be the kind of person that is worthy of such a spouse. Finally, pray that God will protect your purity and thought life for both of you.

MATTHEW

5:14-16

YOU ARE THE LIGHT OF THE WORLD.
A CITY SITUATED ON A HILL CANNOT
BE HIDDEN. NO ONE LIGHTS A LAMP
AND PUTS IT UNDER A BASKET, BUT
RATHER ON A LAMPSTAND, AND IT
GIVES LIGHT FOR ALL WHO ARE IN
THE HOUSE. IN THE SAME WAY, LET
YOUR LIGHT SHINE BEFORE OTHERS,
SO THAT THEY MAY SEE YOUR GOOD
WORKS AND GIVE GLORY TO YOUR
FATHER IN HEAVEN.

SERIOUS COMMITMENT

discover |

READ MATTHEW 5:31-32.

"It was also said, Whoever divorces his wife must give her a written notice of divorce. But I tell you, everyone who divorces his wife, except in a case of sexual immorality, causes her to commit adultery. And whoever marries a divorced woman commits adultery."

No one gets married with plans to be divorced. That would be like saying at the wedding, "until this becomes inconvenient for us both" instead of "until death do us part." In New Testament times, from Old Testament rules, in order for a man to divorce his wife, all he had to do was get two witnesses and quietly write up a divorce. Jesus urged people to take their marriage commitment seriously. Marriage is important to God, and the consequences of a hasty divorce add more pain to everyone involved.

Taking the last few verses together, lust can harm a marriage, and in turn, a harmed marriage can lead to divorce. Very rarely does a person wake up one day and decide they are going to ruin their marriage relationship with divorce. Hardly ever does a person wake up and say, "Today, I think I will commit adultery and destroy my marriage."

Marriages are broken apart by adultery after hundreds of small choices that often begin with things born in the imagination. For Jesus to spend so much time teaching about marriage and sexuality in the Sermon on the Mount means that you should be preparing yourself today for such an important life-long commitment.

delight |

Spend some time thinking about all the people you know who are married. Out of those people, focus on those that you know are trying to honor God with every part of their life. What healthy things do you see in their marriage?

What are some things you could do right now to prepare for your future marriage?

display |

As a student, you can prepare for your future relationships and marriage right now in your friendships, family, and faith community. Encourage everyone you know to honor God through their marriages. As you chase after a pure mind, support those around you to do the same.

Think of one marriage relationship in your family (parents, grandparents, aunts or uncles, etc.) and write them a note or text of encouragement to love God with their marriage. List ways they have modeled for you what a God-honoring marriage looks like. Tell them you are praying for them. This will mean more to them than you will ever know.

If your family doesn't have many examples of healthy marriages, think about someone in your church family who does and do the same exercise. Make sure they know how much their marriage means to you and how much you admire the way they love each other.

> **Since God created marriage and sex, it is important for you to pray for healthy relationships that honor God in this area. Pray for any family, friends, or faith community that you feel led to do so. Pray that God will protect hearts and minds for marriages that will help the world to see the greatness and glory of God. Pray this for yourself especially.**

PROMISE ON BATMAN?

discover |

READ MATTHEW 5:33-37.

"But let your 'yes' mean 'yes,' and your 'no' mean 'no.' Anything more than this is from the evil one."—Matthew 5:37

I have twin daughters. They talk about everything. They share everything. However, when things get serious and they need to know they are telling the full truth, one will ask the other, "Do you promise on Batman?" I don't know why Batman became the highest and most important measure of integrity, but he somehow did.

In the time of Jesus, Rabbis had made regulations regarding oaths so complex that a person's word was not as trustworthy as it should have been. Making promises by swearing or by oath was significant because people had difficulty trusting each other. This is because, in general, people have proven to be untrustworthy.

How many times have people in your life promised things only to fail on that promise? While most people don't do it on purpose, there are some who say things they really don't mean. Sadly, we all do the same thing. How many times have you promised something only to fail at that promise? Like sisters "promising on Batman," we can all agree that most of us struggle with keeping our word.

Jesus called His followers to a higher standard. God is calling us to a higher standard through His Word. Mean what you say, because it matters. Your integrity reflects the faithfulness that God has displayed throughout time and history.

delight |

Have you been guilty of saying yes to someone, knowing full well that you would not follow through on your yes? What needs to happen in your heart for you to be able to say yes and mean it or say no and mean it?

Reflecting on what God has done in the Bible, what does that mean for your level of trust in God today in your life?

display |

Your words must continue to match your actions because that is exactly what Jesus did and what God faithfully continues to do for us. Your actions reflect your faith. But let's take one day at a time. Think about your last 24 hours. How did you keep your word and where did you fall short? Compare this to the 24 hours in front of you. What do you have coming up as an opportunity to grow in small or large matters of integrity? List a few opportunities below.

Pray that God will focus your heart to be consistent and faithful with everyone around you. Pray that God will use your faithfulness for His glory.

DEFENDER

discover |

READ MATTHEW 5:38-42.

"But I tell you, don't resist an evildoer. On the contrary, if anyone slaps you
on your right cheek, turn the other to him also."—Matthew 5:39

If someone were to attack you emotionally or physically, who do you feel would be responsible for protecting you? Give it some thought.

After all the people you just thought of, including yourself, at any point did you consider God as your defender? Christians are called to believe in God as savior, but we rarely think of Him in this way. Why is that? Maybe because other people are physically with us or we have determined that we should take care of ourselves. Jesus thinks differently.

"Eye for an Eye" shows up at least three times in the Old Testament. It is a truly fair regulation. It keeps people from going overboard in anger and offering a fair and measured response to an attack. An example would be: If someone's cow was stolen, the person who stole it would return the cow and then give one of their own cows to know what it felt like to lose property.

Jesus took the feeling of loss and turned it into an opportunity to declare your supreme faith in the God of the universe. The first attack on the cheek is one of disrespect. A person is shaming you by striking you. To defend yourself from this attack would be like protecting your own honor. A second hit would be withstanding pain because of your faith in God. How exactly is this? By not defending yourself, you are trusting God to be your defender and protector. Turning the other cheek is actually a statement of faith.

delight |

How do you think "turning the other cheek" would allow you to honor God through your actions?

Do you consider God the ultimate judge of all things in your life? If so, then how should this affect situations where you feel wronged or attacked?

display |

While no one expects you to go walking around looking for opportunities to get run over in daily life, removing yourself as the true defender of your integrity changes things. It might not be a situation that you can create, but certainly reminding yourself daily that God is the defender of all things—including you— can transform your thinking.

Look up Romans 12:19. Rewrite this verse in your own words in the space provided below:

We all have hurt and pain that has stayed with us. Consider a few deep pains that you currently are struggling with that you would like to trust God with. Consider writing them down, wadding it up in a ball in your hand, and then dropping it in the trash as if to say you are letting go of it and giving that thing to God. Pray for God to help you trust Him as your sole defender and your soul defender.

SACRIFICIAL LOVE

discover |

READ MATTHEW 5:43-48.

"You have heard that it was said, Love your neighbor and hate your enemy. But I tell you, love your enemies and pray for those who persecute you," —Matthew 5:43–44

Love your enemies? This goes against all of our feelings and much of what we are taught outside of the Christian faith. Jesus confirmed this by acknowledging that many felt it was acceptable to hate your enemy. Some even felt the Old Testament taught this idea.

While the direct phrasing "hate your enemy" is not there, if you spend a little time thinking about how God dealt with people that went against Israel or the things of God in the Old Testament, it's not hard to draw the conclusion that many in Jesus's day thought it was okay to hate your enemy. Like always, what Jesus commanded His followers to do was different from how the crowd felt and cut right to the heart of how God feels about people.

The word translated as love in this text is *Agape*. This is different from romantic or brotherly affection. This is self-sacrificial love. This type of love is supposed to be different. It's supposed to look like praying for enemies, doing good for enemies, greeting them, and treating them with human decency. Why would Jesus demand such actions?

Because Jesus willingly laid down His life for the world. He prayed for His enemies. Jesus did much good for people that didn't deserve it, and He went above and beyond to sacrificially love everyone. There is nothing normal or easy about what Jesus calls His followers to do.

delight |

Take a moment and consider people in your life that you may qualify as enemies. Now consider how you specifically have been an enemy to God. If Jesus gave up His life for you and experienced suffering and death, then how can you follow the example of Jesus with these people you have identified as enemies?

What does praying for enemies, doing good, and greeting them look like in your world today?

display |

Praying to God is a declaration of belief that God can change a situation. How can you pray directly for your enemies every day? If they are your enemies, it is possible that they do not live for Christ. By praying for them, you are actively praying for the salvation and transformation of someone who doesn't know Jesus. Beyond this, treating them with kindness and making a plan for how you can do good in their lives shows them the love of Christ. Caring for enemies the way Jesus described is potentially the most life-changing thing you could do for someone else. Use the space below to write a prayer for someone who you might feel is an enemy.

Have you ever really prayed for non-Christians before? Challenge yourself to add to your daily prayer routine to pray for enemies and other people that do not know Jesus. Make it specific. Say names. Allow God to change your heart for some of the people you have the most difficult time with.

SECTION 2

THE HOW

Section two of the Sermon on the mount is all about submission. Essentially, if you love God and have chosen to follow Jesus in faith, you are submitting to Him. When you pray, you are submitting to God. When you follow God rather than your own way—rather than worshiping other things—you are submitting to God. This is how you live out your faith.

SECRET GOOD, ETERNAL REWARD

discover |

READ MATTHEW 6:1-4.

"So whenever you give to the poor, don't sound a trumpet before you, as the hypocrites do in the synagogues and on the streets, to be applauded by people. Truly I tell you, they have their reward."—Matthew 6:2

These few verses have a lot of concepts that are important to understand. Let's explore three—what it means to practice righteousness, hypocrisy, and a crowd. If you don't know, a hypocrite is a person who claims one thing, but does another.

If someone was "practicing righteousness" by helping a person in need but doing it in front of other people, then their motivation can become murky. Are you helping a person because they need it? Are you helping a person because you want to honor God? Or could it be that you are helping a person because you want other people to be impressed by you? If you are only trying to impress other people by what you are doing, then as Jesus said, your reward will only come from the people watching and not from God. He is not interested in wrongly motivated good deeds.

Jesus calls His followers to do the right thing for the purpose of honoring God alone. Not for fame or to receive anything from it, but solely to bring God glory. Anything else would be hypocrisy. Our reward is eternity in heaven with God because of faith in Christ alone. We live differently because of what Jesus has done. That means we help those in need without being recognized for it.

delight |

Think about some "good" things you've done in the past. Why did you do them? Was it because you cared what people thought? Was it because you saw a need and you wanted to help?

Jesus gave His life for the world, knowing it could not repay Him for His gift. How does this gift of grace change you?

display |

Read Matthew 5:16. So which one is it? Are we supposed to let our light shine before others, or are we supposed to help others in secret? Well, it's both! It's clear that Jesus called His disciples to display their good works, but only so that God gets the praise. If our good works are motivated out of a pat on the back for ourselves, we've missed the mark. Our good works are to be to the praise of our Father in heaven. Today, how can you help those in need without getting credit for it and offering the praise to God? Write two ideas below.

Pray that God will show you opportunities to honor Him in word and deed. Ask God to reveal any selfishness within you. Pray for strength to care less about what people think and more about what God is calling you to do for His glory. Pray for boldness to do righteous things in secret.

AUTHENTIC PRAYER

discover |

READ MATTHEW 6:5-8.

"But when you pray, go into your private room, shut your door, and pray to your Father who is in secret. And your Father who sees in secret will reward you." —Matthew 6:6

Jesus spent some time talking about prayer in a way that sounds different from how we think about prayer today. While prayer is a more private thing today, back then, praying was often done in public places in front of crowds. This meant that sometimes people praying enjoyed sounding impressive more than realizing they were speaking with the God of the universe. Most people back then understood they ought to pray, but often became misguided in what they were doing.

Jesus pointed to praying to God with an understanding of authenticity. He compared people who were doing it for all the wrong reasons, and then He taught the correct way. Authentic prayer was explained to be private, personal, and simple. An important part of praying is realizing that you are developing a relationship with God. It has to be real.

Verse 8 perfectly points to a question we all must ask. What's the point of praying at all? If God already knows everything, then why are we praying? Jesus wants His followers to develop a personal relationship of trust and intimacy with God. For anyone that follows Jesus back then or today: God wants you to know Him and trust Him. That type of relationship is forged in prayer.

delight |

A big part of prayer is understanding that God sees you and hears you. How does it make you feel knowing that God knows every detail about you?

There is nothing that you can surprise God with. As Jesus explained, we know that God wants us to pray to Him to talk with Him. If God knows everything, then the purpose of prayer is for you to grow in knowing Him and trusting Him with your life. What are some ways you can be "real" with God when you pray?

display |

The only way to participate in "authentic" prayer is for you to be real. What are some ways that you can make prayer true to yourself and with God? Maybe you need to write out word for word your heart for God to see. Maybe you need to get somewhere that you know no one else can hear you and talk out loud with God. Maybe you have problems focusing and holding your hands up while you pray will cause you to not waste your words and keep you honest about what you are saying. This is between you and God. But the only way to grow in your faith is to practice what Jesus called His disciples to do. What is He calling you to do? Spend some time in authentic prayer today. Choose one of the ideas above or something else entirely. The point is—pray.

Honest. Simple. Real. Challenge yourself to only say or write things down to God that you authentically believe and need to say. What are some things you would never say to anyone else? In holy reverence, talk to God about the honest, simple, and real things today.

The Essentials

THE LORD'S PRAYER

discover |

READ MATTHEW 6:9-13.

*"Therefore, you should pray like this: Our Father in heaven,
your name be honored as holy." —Matthew 6:9*

The Lord's Prayer is famous. A lot of people know it and have never read Scripture. When studied closely, it reveals some powerful truths. The first thing we hear is that Jesus told His disciples to call God both "heavenly" and "Father." God is heavenly in the sense that He is above everything and all-mighty. God is the cosmic creator of the universe. But Jesus also told His disciples to call Him "Father." That's intimate and special. God is both of these things.

"Your name be honored as holy" is a phrase that reminds us that no one is like God. He is completely "other" in category. The God of the universe who is completely separated from everything else wants His followers to call Him "Father."

Another easy thing to skip over is references to God's kingdom and His will. Not so fast. When you pray to God that His kingdom will reign and rule and His will be done, you are declaring God's supreme power over your personal life. Can you really pray those things with authenticity?

Lastly, Jesus taught His followers to spend time asking God for everything in their lives, from salvation to meals showing up for them to eat. Jesus wanted them to pray for everything. This helps us to see and know that God is the ultimate provider.

delight |

Praying like Jesus called His disciples to helps us understand God and know how He wants us to think and what He calls us to do. What do you think God's kingdom means? (You can find some answers in Exodus 19 and 1 Peter 2:9.)

How do you try to live under God's authority and His way every day?

display |

Pick up your Bible. Look through it a bit; anywhere you'd like. Begin creating a list below (or on another sheet of paper) of who God appears to be in Scripture. Write down His characteristics. Then, as you are praying, talk to God about who He is, revealed in Scripture, and how you can trust His will and way because of what the Bible says.

Beside your list of things about God, write down some specific ways you can choose to follow God's will versus your own selfish way. Compare the two lists. As you understand more who God is, allow it to help cultivate your relationship with Him.

Step by step, read and understand each part of the Lord's Prayer. Then, don't pray to God exactly what it says, but instead, pray to God in your words exactly what it means for your life. Try this approach every time you pray. Don't do the same thing every time, but take the points Jesus explained and use them in your own prayers.

FORGIVENESS

discover |

READ MATTHEW 6:14-15.

"For if you forgive others their offenses, your heavenly Father will forgive you as well. But if you don't forgive others, your Father will not forgive your offenses."

Does this passage sound a little "rewards" based to you? It's almost like an "if this, then that" equation. This could not be farther from what Jesus really meant. It's easy sometimes to feel like Christianity is a bunch of rules: that if you follow God just right, He'll forgive you and you get eternity. That is absolutely the opposite of what Jesus taught. Christians are called and compelled to live for God because of what Jesus has done on the cross.

Authentic Christians understand the value of forgiveness. Romans 3:23 reminds us that the entire world has made mistakes that cause us to fall short of God's perfect standard. We have sinned. Romans 6:23 shows us that we deserve death and separation from God because of our sin. We do not deserve forgiveness, yet God gives it to us because of what Jesus has done. Faith in Christ saves us and forgives our sins.

Because Christians understand this gift of grace that is forgiveness, we see the value in forgiving others. Yet every day, we let little things bother us. We hold grudges and we don't want to forgive people that have become our enemies. Sound familiar?

Christians are compelled to forgive because they have been forgiven in the ultimate way. Choosing not to forgive would mean that you really don't understand what God has done through the life, death, and resurrection of Jesus.

delight |

In the last few days, name a few times that you have excused away some sin you have done or in some way excused your sins by blaming others for their actions.

Compare your actions to what Jesus did for you. What anger and unforgiveness are you holding on to that—because of the mercy Jesus has shown—you need to let go of and forgive?

display |

A path to practicing authentic forgiveness is a three step process. 1. Repent. Find out exactly what is wrong, and then own it. Dive deeper behind not just your action of unforgiveness, but specifically why you don't want to forgive. 2. Tell yourself truth from Scripture about who God is and how He forgives. 3. Obey the truths that God calls us to do from His Word. This is how you can move forward in working toward forgiving others. Who do you need to forgive today? Write their name below.

Using the Lord's prayer method we explored on Day 13, how can you pray in a way that will help you practice forgiveness? Combine the three-step process above and see how it matches up with the Lord's prayer. Talk to God about the root of your anger and unwillingness to forgive. Declare to Him the truths you know about God. Finally, ask Him for the strength to take steps of obedience.

The Essentials

WHEN FASTING

discover |

"Whenever you fast, don't be gloomy like the hypocrites. For they disfigure their faces so that their fasting is obvious to people. Truly I tell you, they have their reward." —Matthew 6:16

In these verses, Jesus spoke of how to properly fast. Fasting is abstaining from food or another substance to focus your heart to depend more deeply on God.

Just a few verses before this, Jesus specifically spoke about food in the Lord's Prayer. He taught His disciples to ask for provision for daily bread. Why daily? Because they didn't have refrigerators in Jesus's day. Most people worked for the day and were paid for the day. That day's work provided them with food. Food wasn't laying around in abundance or on ice. Asking for bread meant they were trusting God for all their needs daily.

Today, the opposite can be true. It seems like food can be found just about anywhere and everywhere. Your kitchen can freeze, cool, warm, and microwave all in a matter of seconds. Most have never experienced going without food. Along with water, food is necessary for life. Yet, it's not really something most people think too much about.

When you don't really need food to be provided, it can be easy to fail to remember that it is God who provides everything. Less dependence on God to make it through a day often creates less opportunities to trust God with all things, including what and when we eat. Fasting is a choice that develops your trust and understanding of dependence on God for all things, including food.

delight |

Why does Jesus say, "when you fast"? Because Jesus expected His followers to fast. It was a part of their regular lives. How you feel about your daily dependence on God can greatly improve by making fasting a part of your life. Do you depend on God for everything? How can fasting help you?

If you have fasted before, why did you do it? If you have never fasted, what are your reasons?

The Essentials

display |

There are three things you need to practice when fasting:

1. Make sure you are safe and not causing yourself medical harm in some way by fasting. If you are good to go, you should consider making it a regular part of your life. Maybe for you, that is one day a week. Maybe it's once a month. But Jesus didn't say "if," He said "when."

2. The focus of your fasting needs to revolve around prayer—talking to God at all times, reading Scripture to help you focus your prayer, and every time you feel hunger, devoting time to God to give you strength and depend on Him.

3. Just like the text, this is not a "show" or "tell" kind of thing. It isn't something to brag about or even really let people know about for that matter. This is between you and God for the purpose of growing in dependence on Him.

At some point this week, plan on following these three guidelines and practice fasting.

Spend some time today talking with God about different ways you can depend on Him more. Think about the things you place trust and dependence on over Him and ask for forgiveness. Prayerfully think about how you can take steps of obedience.

HOLDING ON

discover |

READ MATTHEW 6:19-21.

"For where your treasure is, there your heart will be also."—Matthew 6:21

Jesus taught more lessons about money than he did any other social issue. In just a few verses, He went from connecting the importance of depending upon God with food to the world's love of money. Food and money both have interesting results on your faith life. They both deal with value and dependence. Food is something you need to live. Money is something that most people think will make their existence easier.

Money in and of itself is not evil. This passage is not telling Christians that saving or having money is wrong. Money should be handled with proper understanding and care. But verse 19 presents two realities about things—stuff gets old and fades away, and people can cause you harm trying to take your earthly possessions.

Money and things can bring a false sense of security when it comes to daily dependence. If you have a lot of money, sometimes you can begin to depend on your wealth more than trusting God with your life.

Jesus encouraged His disciples to strive for storing up heavenly treasures. This is a figurative way to say all the things He had already taught during the Sermon on the Mount were to value things like sacrificial love, forgiveness, and mercy. If a person invested in heavenly treasures, then the reward would never fade away.

delight

What are a few of your favorite things on earth? Why are they your favorite? For what reasons do you place value on them?

Now, compare your earthly possessions to your relationship with the God of the universe. Think about the eternal gifts God has given you. How do the objects of earth hold up against God's good gifts?

display |

What would the opposite of storing up treasures on earth be? How could you combat the desire to pile up things that will rust and cause harm? The answer is generosity. Christians give out of an overwhelming sense of gratitude for what God has done in their lives. How can you practice generosity so that it will help you to grow in eternal treasures within your heart? Go into your room and see if there are things that you don't use anymore that you can give away. With your parents' permission, start a donation pile and give your unused stuff to someone who needs it.

Taking everything you've learned from the Lord's Prayer to these truths about food, fasting, and money, talk with God about how you can grow in practicing things that are eternal in your life. Ask God for ways you can be led to sacrificially love others. Pray for God to create opportunities for you to be merciful and show forgiveness. Pray for strength to carry out these beautiful gifts God has given to you already.

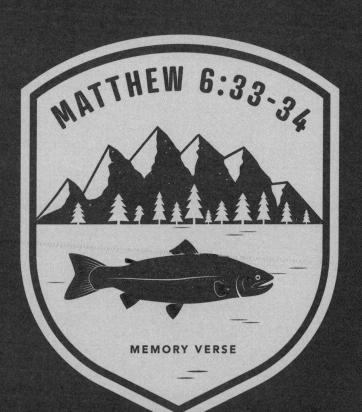

MATTHEW 6:33-34

MEMORY VERSE

But seek first the kingdom of God and his righteousness, and all these things will be provided for you. Therefore don't worry about tomorrow, because tomorrow will worry about itself. Each day has enough trouble of its own.

IN VIEW OF GOD'S MERCY

discover |

READ MATTHEW 6:22-23.

"The eye is the lamp of the body. If your eye is healthy, your whole body will be full of light. But if your eye is bad, your whole body will be full of darkness. So if the light within you is darkness, how deep is that darkness!"

How do things like food and money connect to our eyes? Another way Jesus talked about dealing with eyes was if an eye was causing sin, then you should pluck it out. The eyes seem to matter greatly to our hearts and faith.

If you spend a lot of time looking at food, you'll end up living your life by the demands of your stomach. If you focus on money, it can easily become a false idol in your heart. It is one thing to glance at something; it's another thing to spend time staring at something so much that it becomes an obsession.

Daily provisions and money can create a false sense of security that leads a person to the conclusion that they really don't need God in their life. What you look at and focus on matters.

In Romans 12:1, Paul also taught about the importance of keeping your eyes focused on God. He wrote, "Therefore, brothers and sisters, in view of the mercies of God, I urge you to present your bodies as a living sacrifice, holy and pleasing to God; this is your true worship." It matters what you spend your time viewing. Your eyes could lead you to danger or increase your faith.

delight |

How does focusing on Jesus's life, death, and resurrection cause you to see your life differently?

Does the amount of time you spend with God in prayer impact your perspective on issues you face?

display |

Think about a normal weekday and write down everything you can remember doing while you were awake. What did you do? Additionally, if you have a smart phone, go to the settings menu and find out which apps you spent the most time on. From your entries, make a chart and let your day tell a story. Which things got more focus than God?

No one is perfect, and of course, there are important things we are supposed to do by honoring our parents and working hard at school. However, most of the time, our eyes get fixed on things other than what Jesus has done. Use your chart information to make a plan to change your focus.

> **Read Romans 12:1-2 and make this your prayer to God today. Offer your life, what you do, and what you look at to God in worship. Ask God to forgive you for thoughts that are not pleasing to Him, and ask Him to renew your heart and mind to follow Him. Ask God to help you fix your eyes on Jesus.**

TOTAL DEVOTION

discover |

READ MATTHEW 6:24.

*"No one can serve two masters, since either he will hate one
and love the other, or he will be devoted to one and despise
the other. You cannot serve both God and money."*

It is pretty uncommon for any classroom to have two teachers. Although most teams have a lot of coaches, there is always one coach who is in charge of everything. It wouldn't work with two leaders. This is exactly what Jesus taught in Matthew 6:24. You can't have two leaders pulling you in different directions.

Among the Ten Commandments—laws that God set for Israel to know who God was and how they were supposed to live with each other—God explicitly stated in Exodus 20:3 that, "You shall have no other gods before me." Jesus was also clear in John 14:6 when He said, "I am the way, and the truth, and the life. No one comes to the Father except through me." One way. One God. No others.

Jesus taught about the danger of loving money so much that you end up serving it. There are lots of things you can end up serving and making it your master. Food, money, and material things tend to be the most common examples of things we choose to give our hearts to rather than God.

The reason Jesus spent so much time talking about money was because it tends to be the thing that we often place our trust in more than God. You can't have two masters. God is clear: nothing else can take His place. Jesus was also clear: the only way to true faith in God is through Him.

delight

What are a few other things that you feel like you sometimes serve rather than God?

When you think about your daily activities, where do you find yourself being pulled away from the things of God? What are a few ways you can make some changes?

display |

Let your life be an example of serving God as your one true leader. Going to church is an important aspect of finding other like-minded people to help you take steps of faith. How can you make attending church a higher priority?

Also, being led by the Holy Spirit, seek ways to practice mercy and kindness toward others. This is evidence that your heart belongs to God. What are some specific ways you can practice the love and forgiveness that Jesus has shown you? Let your actions be a reflection of your heart's devotion to God.

Use this prayer time to confess your sins to God in relation to the many ways you have tried to serve masters other than Him. Get detailed. Be specific. This time of confession will help you to be aware of where you stumble and how you can avoid future service to things that cause sin in your life.

EVERYONE WORRIES

discover |

READ MATTHEW 6:25-30.

*"If that's how God clothes the grass of the field, which is here
today and thrown into the furnace tomorrow, won't he do much
more for you—you of little faith?" —Matthew 6:30*

Anxiousness and worry are a big part of everyone's lives these days.
There is a lot of pressure to succeed. Christians can feel pressure to
always do the right thing. Jesus knew that anxiousness was a big part of
how the people in the New Testament lived. Can you imagine what it
would be like to know that if you didn't work one day, you wouldn't get
paid and your family couldn't eat? That is why Jesus talked about food,
money, and worry all in close proximity.

Jesus compared the birds in the air and the grass in the field to people
that followed God. Jesus said that birds never worry about anything.
They don't store food for winter. They fly and eat and somehow continue
to exist. How is this possible? Jesus's answer for this is the God of
the universe. God takes care of the entire spinning world, and yet we
continue to worry about the days to come.

Have you ever thought about what worry actually accomplishes?
Nothing. Imagine being thirteen years old and shorter than everyone
else. Your parents are tall. It starts to really bother you when everyone
is growing and you aren't. So, you start to worry. Do you think that
worrying about getting taller helps you grow? Of course not. Yet, we
do it. The act of worrying or being anxious only brings harm. You are
accomplishing nothing by worrying, yet it takes up so much headspace.
Why is this? The amount of worry in our lives reveals our lack of trust in
our God. "Little faith" in verse 30 actually means that Jesus thinks their
faith is little.

delight |

Giving your life to Jesus means you are a Christian. You have been saved, forgiven, and made right with God. According to Scripture, it means that God sees you as His child. You belong to God. Do you ever find yourself worrying that you aren't good enough for God to love you?

God loves you because you belong to Him. Nothing more. There is nothing you can do to be separated from God's love. God loves you. Completely. Because of this, do not worry about what happens next. How can you put barriers to worry in place for your heart and mind?

The Essentials

display |

Dwelling in God's love helps you to battle anxiousness. If God loves you, it helps you to trust Him. If you trust Him, then you can ask for His will and way to be done in your life. This means, more so than any bird or blade of grass, you can trust God to provide for you. The best way to fight worry is to practice "dwelling" in God. This means that you must work toward making your brain think about God's love and how you can trust Him. Using the word TRUST below, create an acrostic that reminds you of how much God loves you. Use Scripture to support your claims.

T

R

U

S

T

I want to ask you to do something that maybe you haven't thought about in a while. Sing the song, "Jesus Loves Me" to yourself. Make it a prayer. Then think about how from the Sermon on the Mount, this only helps you to be more confident in His love.

SEEK FIRST

discover |

READ MATTHEW 6:31-34.

"But seek first the kingdom of God and his righteousness, and all these things will be provided for you." —Matthew 6:33

Material things, food, the future, and worry are all connected and reveal a significant issue Christians face: we have small faith. We love God and believe in Him, but don't want to hand over all the things we face.

Jesus told His disciples not to worry. That means anxiousness and worry are something you can control. Worry is something you turn on in your mind when you start to imagine things possibly going wrong. What if this headache turns into an illness that is going to cause me to miss school? What if I miss tests and the teacher gives me a zero? What if I can't get into college, won't meet the person of my dreams, and eventually end up a failure in life all because of this headache? It sounds silly when you read it, but it's not that far away from the tricks your mind can play on you and your trust in God. Worry shows small faith.

How do we choose not to worry? By seeking first the kingdom of God and turning our minds to the things God calls us to do daily. The word *daily* is very important. It isn't future-forward. "Daily" reminds you that today is today and tomorrow is another day. You are not in control of tomorrow; God is. In fact, God is in control of today. Jesus called His people to trust God with their todays every day. God calls us to daily trust God and make a choice not to worry.

delight |

Can you name a few things that trigger worry for you? Is it the things coming up in the days, months, and years that you can't predict or control? What makes your mind go into overdrive when it comes to being anxious?

How is God calling you today to seek His kingdom first?

display |

Taking the Sermon on the Mount thus far, let's build a step-by-step plan to put faith into action to combat worry:

1. Remind yourself of all the reasons you love God.

2. Say out loud the ways you want to submit to God's will and way (see day 13).

3. Work on doing things that matter to God and are eternal.

4. Find people around you who are hurting and in need of help, and serve them.

5. Tell other people how Jesus saved you.

6. Repeat these steps for the rest of your life!

One of the best ways we can pray is to memorize Scripture and repeat it in our prayers. Memorize Matthew 6:33 and then talk to God about it. Ask God specifically how you can search out His kingdom every day. Ask God to reveal it to you.

SECTION 3

THE HOPE

In the first section, Jesus dealt with the heart. In the second section, Jesus focused on submission. In this final section, Jesus concludes by comparing the two options everyone has in life: choosing to live for God or choosing to live for self. The option to live selfishly ends in painful destruction. However, a life for Jesus means hope for every believer. It is a life built on the firm foundation of God. This is a great reminder that when life brings difficulty, we are blessed that God is with us.

PLANK VS. SPLINTER

discover |

READ MATTHEW 7:1-5.

"Or how can you say to your brother, 'Let me take the splinter out of your eye,' and look, there's a beam of wood in your own eye?"—Matthew 7:4

This is one of those passages that might get quoted almost as much as John 3:16. It's also often misinterpreted. On the surface, it sounds like a Christian should never judge anyone. That, however, is not what the passage really means.

Jesus was talking about someone condemning another person for their actions but never looking inward at their own sin. It is a terrific thing to allow Scripture and the Holy Spirit to inform your life with truth. But always having a critical heart condemning others for their actions is not God's desire.

Part of being a part of a faith community is helping keep each other accountable. We should always help a fellow Christian in their journey to faithfulness. But Jesus calls us to be mindful of and make sure we are dealing with our personal sin issues first and foremost before we ever focus on anyone else's issues.

It seems much easier to notice the issues that other people are facing rather than deal with our own struggles. This is why Jesus talked about the difference between a plank and a splinter. Personal sin is a giant plank that we all deal with. Other people's issues are not to be our main focus. It is only something we deal with after we've been honest with God about our own battles.

delight |

How does the correct interpretation of this text cause you to see it differently? Why do you think it is easier to focus on other people's shortcomings than on your own problems?

How are you able to see more clearly the issues others face rather than your own?

display |

The best way to practice Matthew 7:1-5's concept of "judge not" is to begin with "self-judging." Take some time each day and evaluate how you are living differently because of Jesus. Don't be afraid to talk with other fellow Christians about your own personal struggles in humility. You know which of your friends are safe and who you can do this with. You know which friends will offer you encouragement, be able to know where you are coming from, and will help you evaluate issues you may be facing. Write the name of a friend like this below and seek them out today to help hold you accountable.

Every time you find yourself facing a critical heart toward others, ask God for forgiveness. Next, spend time talking to God about your own struggles before you begin praying for your friends and other fellow Christians. This sets the order correct: plank first, splinter second.

PIGS WEARING PEARLS?

discover |

READ MATTHEW 7:1-6.

"Don't give what is holy to dogs or toss your pearls before pigs, or they will trample them under their feet, turn, and tear you to pieces."—Matthew 7:6

In Jesus's time, pigs were considered "unclean" or dirty, not safe for people to eat. Dogs were not as much pets as they were wild animals that roamed. It seems out of left field that Jesus would say "don't judge people" in one verse, and then a few verses later call them dogs or pigs. However, Jesus used colorful illustrations before—things like, "if your right hand causes you to sin, cut it off" (Matt. 5:30).

Jesus wasn't calling people names as much as He was trying to help Christians understand the best times and places to share what is precious. In other words, if you had done your soul work and dealt with your plank and then went to someone else and offered to help with their splinter, they might trample your valuable help if they haven't truly submitted to Jesus. It would be like giving a pig some pearls to wear. It's a funny image, but pigs wearing pearls is a complete waste of such beauty.

To offer someone help who wants it is of tremendous value to everyone. To try to offer up eternal help to someone who rejects it can be extremely painful. There are times and places to be bold in your faith, and there are other times when people boldly reject God that we should politely let them be. That is between them and God.

delight |

How much time have you thought about the amazing things that come from God after salvation? As undeserving as everyone is, anyone who follows Jesus in faith will be forgiven and saved. The Bible also says that in Christ, you now have the Holy Spirit within you. One of the jobs of the Holy Spirit is to help you recognize wisdom from God. What are a few more of these things?

Not only do you have wisdom, but God helps you determine how to share His love and when to quietly pray that God will move in power in the lives of others that have rejected Him. It is not your job to judge or defend, only to live as God calls you to. When have you experienced a time when God has made clear that someone is not ready to receive the wondrous free gift He is offering them?

display |

Whenever faced with a situation that might allow you to share what God is doing in your life, or in some other way offer valuable wisdom to others, stop and ask yourself one question: "God, how do you want me to share this truth today?" Attempt to truly listen to the Holy Spirit, and if someone boldly rejects you, practice what Jesus calls us to: turn the other cheek. See it as an opportunity to quietly pray for them in hopes that God will change their hearts.

As you are praying through the Lord's Prayer for God's will and way in your life, also pray that God will save and change people you know—especially the ones who are boldly rejecting Him right now. Pray that they will see God's love in your life and example. Pray that all will come to know Jesus in salvation.

ASK. SEEK. KNOCK.

discover |

READ MATTHEW 7:7-8.

"Ask, and it will be given to you. Seek, and you will find. Knock, and the door will be opened to you. For everyone who asks receives, and the one who seeks finds, and to the one who knocks, the door will be opened."

The Sermon on the Mount is a lot to process. The way Jesus taught created a higher standard for all His disciples, including us today. Jesus's standard was perfection—an impossible task for everyone except Himself.

These few verses should be read together with the rest of the Sermon on the Mount. Think about it this way. In that moment, what Jesus said wasn't perfectly clear to His listeners. To us, we have the good fortune of knowing what came after. We know that Jesus lived up to this standard and never sinned. He then took on the shame and sins of the world and gave up His life on the cross. When God raised Him from the dead, He defeated sin and death and made a way for everyone to be forgiven. What God gives to everyone who seeks is forgiveness and salvation. The thing people were seeking but didn't quite know yet was the gospel: the good news of Jesus Christ.

So in view of what Jesus has said in chapters five, six, and seven, He was saying this: The thing you don't really know you need yet is forgiveness. That means the thing you are seeking is salvation. That is something that God gives to anyone who asks and seeks.

We all fail. We all fall short. God answers anyone who asks for help.

delight |

Spend some time thinking about specific ways you have messed up
the commands that Jesus has given us in the Sermon on the Mount.
Think about ways you've judged others, worshiped other things, and
generally haven't shown forgiveness. Then ask the question: How do
I know that God loves me?

Now, think about God's salvation through Jesus Christ for your life.
Think about how that answers all the questions you ask, seek, and
knock about. How can you delight in the ways God has directly
forgiven you for the things you've failed in?

display |

Asking and seeking are things people do when they don't know what to do. What are some things you can ask God and ways you can seek Him in your daily walk? It may require some humility you have already been practicing with your plank inspections of self examination. Think about ways you can share the good news of what Jesus has done in your heart and life. Share three ways below you can share the good news of what Jesus has done for you with others.

In your moments of devotion today, prayerfully thank God for His salvation in your life. Thank God for saving you from your failures and shame. Thank God for keeping His promises when you couldn't. Thank God for Jesus. Thank God for always answering when you ask, seek, and knock.

FROM GOOD, BE GOOD, DO GOOD

discover |

READ MATTHEW 7:9-12.

"Therefore, whatever you want others to do for you, do also the same for them, for this is the Law and the Prophets."—Matthew 7:12

How does it feel to be called "evil"? Seems harsh. Jesus used dramatic language that is, in every sense, completely accurate. The Bible repeatedly explains that anyone who sins is considered an enemy to God. There are a few places in the New Testament that are interpreted in such a way that our sinful nature is essentially at war with God. It is an undeniable truth that everyone has sinned, and sin separates us from God.

We are capable of good things. Anyone can do something nice. Most of the time, if someone asked for food, we wouldn't hand them a rock. That's the example Jesus gave. Humanity can do lots of good things. Yet, one sin causes disunity with God.

In contrast, God is always good, always right, and never fails. God is perfect. He gave us something we didn't know how to ask for. Jesus was and is God's perfect gift to the world. Here's how all of this fits together with the golden rule (verse 12): God calls us to love others the way we need God to love us. God loved us so much that He sent Jesus. That perfect gift changes our lives for eternity. In response, God wants us to love others in the same way.

God is good. God is good to you. He is calling you to be good to others the way He was good to you.

The Essentials

delight

Read Matthew 22:36-40. What are the similarities between these verses and Matthew 7:12?

While our love isn't perfect like God's, He calls us to love others in a way like He has loved. How can you practice this type of love today?

display |

Make a list of all the ways you wish your friends and family would actually treat you. Think about how you would like to be spoken to, what happens when you mess up, and specific ways they could celebrate you. Now, take some time and think about how you can practice those exact things for other people. This is the golden rule in full effect. Love other people the way you would want to be loved.

> Ask God to remind you what you have been saved from and what your life was like before Christ. Then talk to God about all the ways He's been good to you and good for you. Finally, pray that God will help you love others and do good for them the way God has done good for you.

★ MATTHEW 7:13-14 ★

Enter through the narrow gate. For the gate is wide and the road broad that leads to destruction, and there are many who go through it. How narrow is the gate and difficult the road that leads to life, and few find it.

NARROW PATH, NARROW GATE

discover |

READ MATTHEW 7:13-14.

"Enter through the narrow gate. For the gate is wide and the road broad that leads to destruction, and there are many who go through it. How narrow is the gate and difficult the road that leads to life, and few find it."

Jesus's teaching gave two choices: you could follow the law as written or you could understand the heart of the law. When you pray, are you praying to God or praying for men to hear? Are you interested in worshiping God or money? As with many of Jesus's options, today's verses came down to an illustration of two gates.

Jesus offered the narrow path or the wide path. The narrow path that led to a narrow gate was a difficult choice. The wide path and the wide gate were much easier paths, but the outcome was disastrous.

The narrow path illustration explains what it means to follow Jesus. The way isn't easy because it is a way that requires disciples of Jesus to act like Jesus. God's goodness and salvation are on display through Jesus. Faith in Christ saves you. Because of what God has done in Jesus, Christians are now called to be like Christ. This isn't an easy path. It's narrow. It can be much easier to choose to go the wide path. The wide path that leads to a much wider gate is one of self-pleasure and self idol worship. That selfish path leads to the fullness of separation from God. Destruction.

Which path will you take?

delight

What is the value in the "narrow path"? How are you different from taking the narrow path?

How has your relationship with God changed since you've taken steps toward praying and living the way Jesus calls you to live?

display |

Draw two pictures. One picture is a narrow path with a narrow gate. The other picture is the wide path with the wide gate. Make them as accurate as you'd like. On the wide path, write down all the ways you could follow the crowd, and then at the gate, write down the specific ways it could bring you destruction.

On the narrow path, write down some of the lessons you've learned from the Sermon on the Mount, and then at the gate, write down ways you've experienced new life already.

Stick this picture somewhere you can look at it from time to time to be reminded of the value of taking the narrow path.

Talk with God about all the reasons you have chosen to follow the narrow path. Ask God for strength and courage to continue choosing to love people the way you have been loved in Jesus.

DAY 26

FRUIT

discover |

READ MATTHEW 7:15-20.

"You'll recognize them by their fruit. Are grapes gathered from thornbushes or figs from thistles?"—Matthew 7:16

In the previous few verses, Jesus spoke about a narrow path and a wide path. One led to life; the other, destruction. It's no mistake that Jesus then went on to discuss false teachers. How would someone know if the teacher is false? Jesus said to look for their fruit.

Have you ever found yourself in a place where lots of trees are around? Maybe you've never spent a lot of time wondering what kind of trees are around you, but for the most part, a whole bunch of them can look pretty similar. Brown bark, green leaves, and well, tree-looking. However, if you see apples hanging from the branches, I doubt anyone has ever thought, "Look at that banana tree!"

False teachers would be teaching "wide path/wide gate" type material—things that go against the narrow and difficult teachings of Jesus. That is the type of teaching that many people would enjoy because it sounds good and easy to them. "God wants you to be happy" would be a good example of wide path teaching. The fruit, or result, of such thinking could lead you to a place where it would be much easier to abandon commitments you've made in search of making yourself "more happy." This is a wide path that leads to destruction. Jesus took His illustration in a very serious direction. False teaching and false teachers should be fully rejected. Bad fruit can bring destruction.

delight |

While you probably haven't met someone that labels themself a false teacher, you have definitely spent time with people who share teachings that contradict the words of Jesus. Think about people in your life that have spoken things that directly oppose Scripture. What are some "wide path" teachings that you have experienced? How could they bring harm to you and others spiritually?

What fruit do you see from the false teachings? How do you spot it?

display |

Spiritually speaking, as a tree produces fruit, Christians produce spiritual fruit. Giving our lives to Jesus means that the Holy Spirit dwells within us, and we have evidence of what God has done in our lives. How are you different because of Jesus? What fruit have you experienced? Have you found yourself convicted of sin? Do you hunger for time with God in prayer? Have you found yourself being called to sacrificially love others in a way you didn't expect? How has the Holy Spirit directed you to do good for others? Spend some time thinking about the evidence of your Christian faith. Write out a few examples of the fruit of your life below.

Ask God to help you have wisdom to recognize what you read and hear compared to what Scripture teaches and we believe to be unequivocal truth. Ask God for clarity on "wide path teaching" you might hear and how to avoid anything that pulls you away from the teachings of Jesus.

DO YOU REALLY KNOW?

discover |

READ MATTHEW 7:21-23.

"Not everyone who says to me, 'Lord, Lord,' will enter the kingdom of heaven, but only the one who does the will of my Father in heaven."—Matthew 7:21

Does this Scripture make you nervous? Do you get the strange feeling that maybe you've been doing all these things for God, in His name, yet He might not recognize you when your life comes to an end? That is what makes this text so important for Christians to understand.

In our culture, the general principle is: If you work hard, you will be rewarded for your efforts. This understanding slips into our thoughts about God even though Scripture is very clear about what we deserve (see Rom. 6:23). It doesn't matter how amazing you are at being good. If you sin only once, you have fallen short. Remember Matthew 5:20? "For I tell you, unless your righteousness exceeds that of the scribes and Pharisees, you will never enter the kingdom of heaven."

Sin separates us from God. Good works do not make up for sin. Serving God does not make up for sin. Doing miraculous things in God's name does not make up for sin. The only thing that saves you is faith in Jesus Christ—true, authentic, and genuine faith in Jesus. Faith is how you know He knows you.

Faith in Jesus means truly submitting your life to God. Only admitting that you are a sinner in need of saving and asking God to save you brings salvation. Only that brings transformational change. Christians do good works because of what Jesus has done. This is the fruit from our spiritual tree.

---

delight |

Is it possible that you do lots of good things that you think God will like so He'll love you and let you into heaven? How can today's Scripture help change your mind and heart about this matter?

The most important part of Matthew 7:21 is that Jesus wants your heart, not your works. How can you live in a way that expresses your understanding of this truth more vividly?

display |

Jesus described people doing powerful public works who did not truly follow God. Today, focus on God's will for your life. How do you know God's will? You've been reading about it in this devotional. Jesus gave direct teachings on what God wants you to do with your life. He wants you to give your heart to Him. Your heart in how you live and love. Your heart in how you pray. Jesus wants your heart. Have you given your heart to Jesus? If you have, let the way you practice God's will be in the secret place of prayer and your inner being, overflowing into how you live your outward life. Draw a heart below and write a note to God in it expressing the way you desire to give Him your heart.

The only way to put out the fear of God not knowing you at the day of judgment is truly giving your life to Jesus. If you have never really done that, today could be the day you pray to God and ask for His salvation. If you are a Christian, thank Him for His gracious gift of knowing Him through faith.

DAY 28

ROCK BUILDING

discover |

READ MATTHEW 7:24–25.

"Therefore, everyone who hears these words of mine and acts on them will be like a wise man who built his house on the rock. The rain fell, the rivers rose, and the winds blew and pounded that house. Yet it didn't collapse, because its foundation was on the rock."

Don't miss the progression that Jesus explained. The first goal is to hear and understand the words of Jesus. The second is to practice the words of Jesus with a life of faith. It is one thing to hear something and think it's nice. It's another to apply truth to living. Jesus wants Christians to be both hearers and doers. Living this out means you are a building on a rock-solid foundation.

Sandbox building is precarious. One slip of the shovel or step in the wrong place and all your hard work can come crashing down. But building on firm ground is a much nicer experience. The way Jesus spoke about this foundation is different. He didn't say, "Build your house on whatever rock you can find." He called it "the rock." I wonder what the crowds thought of this phrase when Jesus said it for the first time. He didn't explain it in the moment, but later on in Matthew 16:17-18, He said after Peter (also called Simon) confessed Jesus is the Messiah,"Blessed are you, Simon son of Jonah, because flesh and blood did not reveal this to you, but my Father in heaven. And I also say to you that you are Peter, and on this rock I will build my church, and the gates of Hades will not overpower it." The rock Jesus was referring to is the declaration of faith. Peter believed that Jesus is the Messiah, and Jesus proclaimed that the church will grow because of Peter's example of hearing and doing.

delight |

What are some teachings of Jesus that you hear and understand and have chosen to take action on? How have the results of hearing and doing helped you to be on a firm foundation?

What are some teachings of Jesus you find difficult to follow? What do you need to understand to take action today?

display |

Let's get constructive. Find a location that would be a hard place to build something, like the side of a hill or on an uneven, rocky place. If you have sand nearby, add it to the mix. Then, take whatever is around your home and try to construct a house of sorts. If it's solo cups, then stack them as best you can. If you've got old school wooden blocks, try that. After it's built, pour some water on the "house" and see what happens to the thing you've built.

After your little experiment, consider what it means to build your faith foundation upon Jesus and how secure and safe He is.

> **Ask God to remind you of all the ways He is the rock in your spiritual and physical world. Talk with Him about some rains you've faced and how thankful you are that He has you in His hands no matter what comes your way.**

NOT "IF" BUT "WHEN"

discover |

READ MATTHEW 7:26–27.

*"But everyone who hears these words of mine and doesn't act
on them will be like a foolish man who built his house on the
sand. The rain fell, the rivers rose, the winds blew and pounded
that house, and it collapsed. It collapsed with a great crash."*

Have you ever thought about what sand actually "was"? Sand is just
smaller rocks that couldn't stand up to force of the waves and storms
that crashed into them. The constant abuse caused the rocks to break
apart to a granular level.

Jesus is the unbreakable rock. No storm or wave can break Him down.
This is a great analogy for comparing the truth that comes from Jesus
versus other versions of "truth" that comes from the world. It just doesn't
stand up to the storms of life.

Did you notice that Jesus spoke with certainty when it comes to
the rains, rivers, and winds that will blow and pound? It's not an "if"
proposition, but a "when." The fact that difficulty happens to everyone is
a guaranteed fact of life. Following Jesus or not following Jesus doesn't
change the fact that bad stuff happens. This is part of being in a "fallen"
world (a world corrupted by sin). Jesus doesn't come to protect us from
difficulty. He helps our foundation to be rock solid when storms hit.

The last words of Jesus's Sermon on the Mount came by describing
what happens to people who build their house on the sand. A great fall.
Destruction to everything that was built. What is your life built on?

delight |

As with almost every lesson Jesus taught, you are now faced again with two choices: building your life on the foundation of faith in Jesus Christ or building your life on a foundation of living for yourself. One life stands up to whatever comes its way. The other is built on millions upon millions of rocks that were destroyed by the pressures of this world. It sounds easy when you think about that way. However, the desire to live for ourselves can be overwhelming at times. What will you choose? How will you live it out?

How would you describe to a friend the difference between living your life on the foundation of Jesus versus the crumbling foundation of the world?

display |

Over the last several days, you have been reading and hopefully applying this devotional that contains undeniable truth from God. This has been you building a life on The Rock. You can't ever predict when a storm will come and the rain will fall, but chances are, something has happened that has tested your commitment to Jesus. How has your life stood up to the challenges you've faced? How do you see evidence of God's grace and strength helping you to stand up under difficulty? Write about these things below.

Prayerfully consider what it means to have a foundation of faith and what it felt like before Jesus. Talk with God about your gratitude for His goodness. Pray for other people who you may feel are creating lives on top of sand. Ask God for His saving power to happen in their lives.

DAY 30

TRUE AUTHORITY

discover |

READ MATTHEW 7:28–29.

When Jesus had finished saying these things, the crowds were astonished at his teaching, because he was teaching them like one who had authority, and not like their scribes.

The Sermon on the Mount has been piling truth upon truth for us. The message Jesus gave was revolutionary, yet the most surprising thing was that none of it was particularly new. All the truths He preached about, God had revealed to the people of Israel before. The crowds of that day were amazed or astonished by what Jesus had to say because He spoke with such authority.

God's Word from beginning to end is accurate, consistent, and does not contradict itself. Jesus proved that by explaining the Ten Commandments in proper context. Even more so, He revealed just how impossible it would be to keep them all perfectly. This highlighted the world's need for salvation. Jesus knew why He was on Earth.

The disciple John called Jesus "The Word." In every way, Jesus is the fulfillment of the promises God gave to Abraham, Moses, and David; promises to bless the world by giving a Messiah. God kept His word. Jesus was the Word. John says "The Word became flesh and dwelt among us" (John 1:14).

What Jesus said had and has authority. What Jesus did provided salvation for the world. He lived the Sermon on the Mount perfectly, exceeding all the scribes and prophets. His sacrifice on the cross was taking punishment for sin, which He did not deserve. He kept God's promise for the world and us.

The Essentials

delight |

Flip back through this book an take a look at everything you've learned from Jesus and His sermon in Matthew 5-7. What was your favorite lesson you've learned? How have you begun to apply many of these concepts to your life?

Because of what Jesus has done, are you more willing to forgive and love than before? How has this been made evident in your life?

display |

Jesus challenged everyone that heard His message to not only hear, but do. As you think about where you are today versus where you were before you began hearing and doing the Sermon on the Mount, do you see God's powerful truths at work? Do you see a difference in who you were versus how you think and act today?

Write down some ways you find yourself amazed by God's truth and how it has changed not just you, but the way you treat others.

Just as the crowd recognized Jesus's authority by how He taught, spend your time praying about God's authority in your personal life. Lay down all of your hopes and dreams at His feet and ask Him to be in charge of everything. Ask forgiveness for the ways you've fallen short and ask God to help you to take steps of faith recognizing the authority He has in your life.

A LITTLE UPSIDE DOWN

The way we live reveals what's important to us, and what's important to us reveals what we believe to be true. Scrolling through social media on any platform or a glance at the latest news shows what the world generally values and believes. As Christians living in this world yet being set apart for God, it can be incredibly difficult to live differently while remaining compassionate and real with the people around us. Honestly, it can be so tough to know how to answer the questions of what's most important. But this is essential to standing firm in our faith.

How would you say your life answers the question of what's most important to you or what you believe?

Fill in this triangle with what you believe is most important to most people in our society today. The tip of the triangle should be the most important thing. Ideas could include: wealth, popularity/influence, name brands, followers, fame, activism, tolerance, and so on.

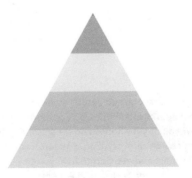

Next, thinking back on what Jesus taught in the Sermon on the Mount, fill in the triangle with what He said was important. This time, the base (biggest section) of the triangle will be what's most important. Ideas include: glorifying God, serving others, obeying God's Word, loving those who can give you nothing in return, and so forth.

Now, mentally flip the triangles. (Or draw them side by side on a separate sheet of paper.) How do they compare?

Even when Jesus walked the earth, His ministry was a little upside down in society's eyes. Material wealth wasn't important to Him. Being popular wasn't important to Him. He didn't need to know the who's who. We never see Him say anything about what clothes to wear or brands to buy—other than to say not to worry because God will provide what we need. He loved God above all and considered the eternal state of others' souls more important than His own life. And He called us to live this way too. Take a minute to let that sink in.

Now, look back at the question you answered at the beginning of this activity about what's important to you. On a separate sheet of paper, draw your own upside down triangle. Fill it in with what you want your life to reveal as most important, with the most important thing listed in the base. Then, spend some time in prayer, asking God to help you live out the reality of His upside down kingdom. Tape this paper to your bedroom door or place it somewhere else you'll see it regularly. Each time you see it, let it be a reminder that God calls us to live a little upside down.

THE HEART:
THE ROOT OF IT ALL

Jesus started this most famous of sermons by focusing on the heart. The Greek word for heart found in Matthew 5:8 is *kardia*, which can mean your physical heart (which circulates the blood throughout your body) or the spiritual seat of our souls; the very center of who we are, where our will, emotions, and thoughts find their root. We also know our words and actions come from the heart (see Matt. 12:34; Luke 6:45). Sometimes, facing what's on the inside—the parts of us that no one sees—can be scary. But it's a good and necessary part of growing with Jesus. So, step by step, let's take a look at our hearts.

Step 1: Ask the Holy Spirit to guide you as you examine your thoughts, words, and actions and what they say about what's in your heart.

Step 2: Notice what you think, say, and do throughout the day. Jot down two thoughts that keep popping up—good or bad.

Circle or highlight the word(s) that best describe the overall tone of the words you use.

Kind   **Pessimistic**   *Hopeful*

Angry   *Encouraging*   **SPITEFUL**

Life-giving   Apathetic   **Joyful**

Sarcastic   Other: _____

Describe three actions you took that are pretty typical for you.

1.

2.

3.

Step 3: After examining your thoughts, words, and actions for the day, spend some time in prayer. If the Holy Spirit convicted you of some sin in your life, confess it. If you felt like you were really focused on the Lord and living as He called you to, thank Him for working in your life and pray that you continue to follow Him in humility. If the Holy Spirit revealed to you something to do or give up to bring you closer to God, commit to doing that.

The point of this exercise is not shame—you're human. God knows you are going to mess up. But He also sent Jesus to cover your mistakes and your shame. If your answers here convicted you, don't be discouraged. Instead, use this as a chance to lead you to press into Jesus as you keep going in the same direction, shift course completely, or make changes along the way.

NOTES